W9-ASO-516
AUG 1983
RECEIVED
OHIO DOMINICAN
COLLEGE LIBRARY
COLUMBUS, OHIO
43219

Dont forget to fly

Also collected by Paul B. Janeczko

POSTCARD POEMS

Bradbury Press   Scarsdale, New York

Dont forget to fly

a cycle
of modern poems
collected by
Paul B. Janeczko

 Manufactured in the United States of America. 3 2 1 83 82 81 The text of this book is set in 12 pt. Sabon.

Library of Congress Cataloging in Publication Data
Main entry under title:
Dont forget to fly.
Includes index.
Summary: An anthology of modern poems touching on such phenomena as parents, love, suicide, dentists, poets, insomnia, marriage, Sundays, cemeteries, and cats.
1. American poetry—20th century. 2. Children's poetry, American.
[1. American poetry—Collections] I. Janeczko, Paul B.
PS613.D6 811'.5'08 81-10220
ISBN 0-87888-187-5 AACR2

This book is for Nadine with love
(and cole slaw)
because she showed me how
not to measure love or flour.
From her, too, I learned
that being there is more important
than simply getting there on time.

Contents

&

&

&

&

&

&

&

Dont forget to fly

NOW LIFT ME CLOSE

Now lift me close to your face till I whisper,
What you are holding is in reality no book,
    nor part of a book;
It is a man, flush'd and full-blooded—it is I—
    So long!
—We must separate awhile—Here! take from my lips
    this kiss;
Whoever you are, I give it especially to you;
So long!—And I hope we shall meet again.

—*Walt Whitman*

DAYBREAK

At dawn she lay with her profile at that angle
Which, when she sleeps, seems the carved
  face of an angel.
Her hair a harp, the hand of a breeze follows
And plays, against the white cloud of the pillows.
Then, in a flush of rose, she woke,
  and her eyes that opened
Swam in blue through her rose flesh that dawned.
From her dew of lips, the drop of one word
Fell like the first of fountains: murmured
"Darling," upon my ears the song of the first bird.
"My dream becomes a dream," she said, "come true.
I waken from you to my dream of you."
Oh, my own wakened dream then dared assume
The audacity of her sleep. Our dreams
Poured into each other's arms, like streams.

—*Stephen Spender*

EARLY MORNING

The solitary egret
in a field of new barley.

I think of the loneliness
of angels—lacking even
the body of a shadow
to share.

—*Philip Dow*

&

SONG

Morning opened
Like a rose,
And the snow on the roof
Rose-color took.
Oh, how the street
Toward light did leap!
And the lamps went out.
Brightness fell down
From the steeple clock
To the row of shops
And rippled the bricks
Like the scales of a fish,
And all that day
Was a fairy tale
Told once in a while
To a good child.

—*Donald Justice*

&

A DAY BEGINS

A headless squirrel, some blood
oozing from the unevenly
chewed-off neck

lies in rainsweet grass
near the woodshed door.
Down the driveway

the first irises
have opened since dawn,
ethereal, their mauve

almost a transparent gray,
their dark veins
bruise-blue.

—Denise Levertov

POEM FOR A SUICIDE

After it happened
the doctors would not let me see her
but kept her wrapped up in blankets
because they didn't understand
the greatness of the event

because
they only knew why she had died
not how she had come to this.

After turning to the world
for what it owed her hands
but would not give
she turned to herself
who had nothing to give
her empty desolated
hands made a gift of that
something
wrapped up in blankets.

—*George Economou*

&

ALONG THE RIVER

They had pulled her out of the river. She was dead,
Lying against the rhododendrons sewn with spider's thread.
An oldish woman, in a shabby dress, a straggling stocking,
A worn, despairing face. How could the old do such a thing?

Now forty years have passed. Again I recall that poor
Thing laid along the River Leam, and I look once more.

They have pulled her out of the river. She is dead,
Lying against the rhododendrons sewn with spider's thread.
A youngish woman, in a sodden dress, a straggling stocking,
A sad appealing face. How can the young do such a thing?

—*D. J. Enright*

&

SUICIDE'S NOTE

The calm,
Cool face of the river
Asked me for a kiss.

—*Langston Hughes*

ABANDONED FARMHOUSE

He was a big man, says the size of his shoes
on a pile of broken dishes by the house;
a tall man too, says the length of the bed
in an upstairs room; and a good, God-fearing man,

says the Bible with a broken back
on the floor below the window, dusty with sun;
but not a man for farming, say the fields
cluttered with boulders and the leaky barn.

A woman lived with him, says the bedroom wall
   papered with lilacs and the kitchen shelves
covered with oilcloth, and they had a child,
says the sandbox made from a tractor tire.
Money was scarce, say the jars of plum preserves
and canned tomatoes sealed in the cellar-hole,
and the winters cold, say the rags in the window
   frames.
It was lonely here, says the narrow gravel road.

Something went wrong, says the empty house
in the weed-choked yard. Stones in the fields
say he was not a farmer; the still-sealed jars
in the cellar say she left in a nervous haste.
And the child? Its toys are strewn in the yard
like branches after a storm—a rubber cow,
a rusty tractor with a broken plow,
a doll in overalls. Something went wrong, they say.

—*Ted Kooser*

&

GONE

Wind rattles the apples.
The sky brims with sunset cider.
Field flowers, ash and maples,
dip like flags to the day's close.

No one gathers the wash.
No mice tattoo the cupboards.
There is no house with doors
springing to keep out flies.

Stones in the high weeds
mark where there was.

—*Ralph Pomeroy*

BOY WANDERING IN SIMMS' VALLEY

Through brush and love-vine, well blooded
   by blackberry thorn
Long dry past prime, under summer's late molten light
And past the last rock-slide at ridge-top and stubborn,
Raw tangle of cedar, I clambered, breath short and spit
   white

From lung depth. Then down the lone valley,
called Simms' Valley still,
Where Simms, long back, had nursed a sick wife till she
died.
Then turned out his spindly stock to forage at will,
And took down his twelve-gauge, and simply
lay down by her side.

No kin they had, and nobody came just to jaw.
It was two years before some straggling hunter sat
down
On the porch-edge to rest, then started to prowl. He
saw
What he saw, saw no reason to linger,
so high-tailed to town.

A dirt-farmer needs a good wife to keep a place trim,
So the place must have gone to wrack with his old lady
sick.
And when I came there, years later, old furrows were
dim,
And dimmer in fields where grew maples and such,
a span thick.

So for years the farm had contracted:
now barn down, and all
The yard back to wilderness gone, and only
The house to mark human hope, but ready to fall.
No buyer at tax-sale, it waited, forgotten and lonely.

I stood in the bedroom upstairs, in lowering sun,
And saw sheets hung spiderweb-rotten, and blankets a
 mass
Of what weather and leaves from the broken window
 had done,
Not to mention the rats. And thought what had there
 come to pass.

But lower was sinking the sun. I shook myself,
Flung a last glance around, then suddenly
Saw the old enameled bedpan, high on a shelf.
I stood still again, as the last sun fell on me,

And stood wondering what life is, and love,
 and what they may be.

—Robert Penn Warren

THE DRESSMAKER'S DUMMY AS SCARECROW

On the hillside's upper garden a dressmaker's dummy
Is set among carrot and cress.
No longer can she swivel
In rooms that faces have panelled, eyeballs lit,
Informing stuff with her articulate line;

For an outside world she now stands sentinel
Against the crows, the shy
Foraging rodents who patter
By crisscross paths near by.

There is at times a blindspot in our view
When one sees nothing, is nothing, cannot see
How one has drifted here;
At that breaking-point, one is out of place
As a dressmaker's dummy left there under the sky:
Outside, she is her livery, but changed,
Apart, surrounded by garden; the fern
At the end of perspective
Reaches now to her shoulder;
The moles are wiser and the crows are older;
She may, or she may not, outlast the winter—
The spring may find her still, and grow towards her.

—Barbara Howes

&

ODE TO A DRESSMAKER'S DUMMY

O my coy darling, still
You wear for me the scent
Of those long afternoons we spent,
The two of us together,
Safe in the attic from the jealous eyes
Of household spies
And the remote buffooneries of the weather;

So high,
Our sole remaining neighbor was the sky,
Who, often enough, at dusk,
Leaning her cloudy shoulders on the sill,
Used to regard us with a bored and cynical eye.

How like the terrified,
Shy figure of a bride
You stood there then, without your clothes,
Drawn up into
So classic and so strict a pose
Almost, it seemed, our little attic grew
Dark with the first charmed night of the honeymoon.
Or was it only some obscure
Shape of my mother's youth I saw in you,
There where the rude shadows of the afternoon
Crept up your ankles and you stood
Hiding your sex as best you could?—
Prim ghost the evening light shone through.

—Donald Justice

SEPARATION

Each day
ungently leads
into the night:
a rose unopened,
blackened by the cold.

—*P. Wolny*

&

DISINTEGRATION

the day after you left
things began to break down
as if they were trying
to tell me something

first the cooler died
without warning
and the dogs accused me
of causing the heat

then it rained
and the roof leaked
so I waded through empty rooms
learning that a mop
speaks only to a bucket
and a bucket speaks to no one

this morning
after the dishwasher drowned
in its own soapy water
all the eggs
fell out of the refrigerator
and lay on the floor
staring up at me
with their broken eyes

now I feel the old
pain in my hip
which has returned and moved in
to take your place

soon the valves of my body
will begin to falter
the intricate webs
of my muscles will unweave
while my teeth slowly loosen
and the lines
on my face go astray

but I would have been
no use without you anyway
what good is one shoe

—Richard Shelton

&

GOING IN

Every day alone whittles me.
I go to bed unmated and wake
with a vulture perched on my chest.

I suck my solitude
like a marrow bone, nothing
left but a memory of feasts.

Wait in the silence, wait
empty as a cracked eggshell
for the beating of heavy fast wings

the soft pad of the big cat
the dry grate of scales sliding over rock
the boiling of the waves as he breaches.

I wait for the repressed, the unnamed,
the familiar twisted masks of early
terrors, or what I have always really known

lurks behind the door at night groping
from the corner of my eye, what breaks
through the paper hoop of sleep.

When all of my loves fall from me
like clothing, like the sweet flesh, what
stands but the bones of my childhood

ringed like a treetrunk with hunger
and glut, the tortured gaping
grin of my adolescence homely

as death. Then my bones drop away
like petals, my bones wither
and scatter and still I am waiting

empty as a grey arching sky, waiting
till I fall headlong into my center
the great roaring fiery heart

the crackling terrible furnace of the sun.

—Marge Piercy

THREE MOMENTS

1.
Since you have gone
my heart has become no larger
than a touch   My days are as
moments   I peer cautiously
through the door
I see only the sun

It is hard   This waiting
Since you have gone

2.
Because I can no longer hold you
Because your words cannot contain my name
Because you are far away   forever   from me
Because other voices now fall on my ears

Do you suppose
you are less to me than before

3.
Where has the summer gone?
    It has faded into the clouds

Where has the night gone?
    It has dissolved into the trees

Where has my lover gone?
    Hidden   Hidden behind the flower
    of the moon

—*Susan Sherman*

LOVE LETTER

it has snowed
on this page
and there are tracks
as of a small
animal lost
in the white weather

in the cold battle
of breath
yours forms
the only cloud
on which I can rest
my head

—Linda Pastan

LOVE LETTERS, UNMAILED

Your hand
brushes my hair
and little bells
jump
in the air startling
me so that I
cling to you for fear of
falling up into the sky.

The touch of
your fingers
grazing mine
delicate as
a single drop of wine
in a crystal goblet.
Rolling it round,
I savor it
on my tongue,
try to
make it last
forever.

The words
I
love
you
form
in the air
and melt.

Your palm
against
my cheek,
light as
a snowflake.

—*Eve Merriam*

&

BURNING LOVE LETTERS

1.
Fire that cancels all that is
Devours paper and pen,
And makes of the heart's histories
A cold hearth warm again.
I could as well consume a branch,
Blank paper or black coal
That now, in ashy avalanche,
Scatters the heart whole.

2.
What words led to the end of words?
Coldly, all separate sighs
Shiver in flame, flying upwards,
Merged into burnt lies.
In somersaults of light, words burn
To nothingness, then roll
In dead scrolls, delicate as fern,
Or hiss like a waterfall.

3.
From partial feast to total fast,
From object to mirage,
An animal that cannot last
Appears in fire's cage:
Love's crazy dog in a cold sweat,
Far from its neighborhood,
Circles the puzzle of regret,
On fire in the wood.

4.
Love's ashes lie and will not rise
As fire dies to a black sun
And makes of the heart's histories
A warm hearth cold again.
Cremation's scattered dust confronts
Dead vision, and in these
Ashes I write your name once,
Bending on cold knees.

—*Howard Moss*

TO MY FATHER

May the Milky Way enter my Father's fading eyes in which, as a child, I journeyed across seas as white and blue as those at the Great Poles.

May sunlight find its house in his smile.
May clocks dance in his heart.
May roses bloom in his wine.
May hollyhocks climb his chair.
May the telephone sing him songs.
May lettuce amuse his lips.

May gardens send him engraved invitations to their openings.
May darkness when it unfolds
presage only a field of stars.

—*Ralph Pomeroy*

SONNET FOR MY FATHER

Father, since always now the death to come
Looks naked out from your eyes into mine,
Almost it seems the death to come is mine
And that I also shall be overcome,
Father, and call for breath when you succumb,
And struggle for your hand as you for mine
In hope of comfort that shall not be mine
Till for this last of me the angel come.
But, father, though with you in part I die
And glimpse beforehand that eternal place
Where we forget the pain that brought us there,
Father, and though you go before me there,
Leaving but this poor likeness in your place,
Yet while I live, you cannot wholly die.

—*Donald Justice*

THOSE WINTER SUNDAYS

Sundays too my father got up early
and put his clothes on in the blueblack cold,
then with cracked hands that ached
from labor in the weekday weather made
banked fires blaze. No one ever thanked him.

I'd wake and hear the cold splintering, breaking.
When the rooms were warm, he'd call,
and slowly I would rise and dress,
fearing the chronic angers of that house,

Speaking indifferently to him,
who had driven out the cold
and polished my good shoes as well.
What did I know, what did I know
of love's austere and lonely office?

—*Robert Hayden*

LETTER TO A DEAD FATHER

Five years since you died and I am
better than I was when you were living.
The years have not been wasted.
I have heard the harsh voices
of desert birds who cannot sing.

Sometimes I touched the membrane
between violence and desire
and watched it vibrate.
I learned that a man
who travels in circles
never arrives at exactly the same place.

If you could see me now
side-stepping triumph and disaster,

still waiting for you to say *my son*
my beloved son. If you could only see
me now, you would know I am stronger.

Death was the poorest subterfuge
you ever managed, but it was permanent.
Do you see now that fathers
who cannot love their sons
have sons who cannot love?
It was not your fault
and it was not mine. I needed
your love but I recovered without it.
Now I no longer need anything.

—Richard Shelton

THE SOUND OF NIGHT

And now the dark comes on, all full of chitter noise.
Birds huggermugger crowd the trees,
the air thick with their vesper cries,
and bats, snub seven-pointed kites,
skitter across the lake, swing out,
squeak, chirp, dip, and skim on skates
of air, and the fat frogs wake and prink
wide-lipped, noisy as ducks, drunk
on the bloozy black, gloating chink-chunk.

And now on the narrow beach we defend ourselves from
dark.
The cooking done, we build our firework
bright and hot and less for outlook
than for magic, and lie in our blankets
while night nickers around us. Crickets
chorus hallelujahs; paws, quiet
and quick as raindrops, play on the stones
expertly soft, run past and are gone;
fish pulse in the lake; the frogs hoarsen.

Now every voice of the hour—the known,
the supposed, the strange,
the mindless, the witted, the never seen—
sing, thrum, impinge, and rearrange
endlessly; and debarred from sleep we wait
for the birds, importantly silent,
for the crease of first eye-licking light,
for the sun, lost long ago and sweet.

By the lake, locked black away and tight,
we lie, day creatures, overhearing night.

—Maxine Kumin

&

NIGHTFALL

The mist-foot man who forms within my cellars,
Steals fog-like from my drains, to stalk my slums,
Unguessed by those who stroll my boulevards;

The midnight man who rises at my nightfalls,
Walks in my sleep, takes substance from my shadows,
To stand beyond my street-lamps, dressed in dark,

Stirs again, creeps up his secret stair.

Is he my shadow, or am I his mask?
Which of us is the real? In dread to know

I drive him to his dungeon-pits, where I
Myself fall prisoner, while he keeps the key.

I cannot rise till he ascends his towers,
I move in darkness till he finds his light.

—Elder Olson

&

GOING TO SLEEP IN THE COUNTRY

The terraces rise and fall
As the light strides up and rides over
The hill I see from my window.
The spring in the dogwood now,
Enlarging its small preconceptions,
Puts itself away for the night.
The mountains do nothing but sit,
Waiting for something to happen—
Perhaps for the sky to open.

In the distance, a waterfall,
More sound than vision from here,
Is weighing itself again,
A sound you can hardly hear.
The birds of the day disappear,
As if the darkness were final.
The harder it is to see,
The louder the waterfall.

And then the whippoorwill
Begins its tireless, cool,
Calm, and precise lament—
Again and again and again—
Its love replying in kind,
Or blindly sung to itself,
Waiting for something to happen.

In that rain-prickle of song,
The waterfall stays its sound,
Diminishing like a gong
Struck by the weakening hand
Of a walker walking away,
Who is farther away each time,
Until it is finally dumb.
Each star, at a different depth,
Shines down. The moon shines down.
The night comes into its own,
Waiting for nothing to happen.

—*Howard Moss*

THIS IS A POEM TO MY SON PETER

this is a poem to my son Peter
whom I have hurt a thousand times
whose large and vulnerable eyes
have glazed in pain at my ragings
thin wrists and fingers hung
boneless in despair, pale freckled back
bent in defeat, pillow soaked
by my failure to understand.
I have scarred through weakness
and impatience your frail confidence forever

because when I needed to strike
you were there to be hurt and because
I thought you knew
you were beautiful and fair
your bright eyes and hair
but now I see that no one knows that
about himself, but must be told
and retold until it takes hold
because I think anything can be killed
after a while, especially beauty
so I write this for life, for love, for
you, my oldest son Peter, age 10,
going on 11.

—Peter Meinke

TO MY DAUGHTER

Bright clasp of her whole hand around my finger,
My daughter, as we walk together now.
All my life I'll feel a ring invisibly
Circle this bone with shining: when she is grown
Far from today as her eyes are far already.

—Stephen Spender

TO L. B. S.

Sometimes, tired, I imagine your death:
By childish illness, reasonless accident
Stopped still forever, gone; until I loathe
Fool dramatizations of the brain—I won't.
Thought I could, write them into pictures here.

My child, outlive me! Stay beyond my times
Which—how I see now—could be worse than these,
As they are worse for many who had sons.
Death I can bear for myself once, not twice.
I am out of bed at midnight to beg this.

—Winfield Townley Scott

BOUQUETS

One flower at a time, please
however small the face.

Two flowers are one flower
too many, a distraction.

Three flowers in a vase begin
to be a little noisy

Like cocktail conversation,
everybody talking.

A crowd of flowers is a crowd
of flatterers
(forgive me).

One flower at a time. I want
to hear what it is saying.

—*Robert Francis*

DANDELIONS

These golden heads, these common suns
Only less multitudinous
Than grass itself that gluts
The market of the world with green,
They shine as lovely as they're mean,
Fine as the daughters of the poor
Who go proudly in spangles of brass;
Light-headed, then headless, stalked for a salad.

Inside a week they will be seen
Stricken and old, ghosts in the field
To be picked up at the lightest breath,
With brazen tops all shrunken in
And swollen green gone withered white.

You'll say it's nature's price for beauty
That goes cheap; that being light
Is justly what makes girls grow heavy;
And that the wind, bearing their death,
Whispers the second kingdom come.
—You'll say, the fool of piety,
By resignations hanging on
Until, still justified, you drop.
But surely the thing is sorrowful,
At evening, when the light goes out
Slowly, to see those ruined spinsters,
All down the field their ghostly hair,
Dry sinners waiting in the valley
For the last word and the next life
And the liberation from the lion's mouth.

—Howard Nemerov

WIND FLOWERS

There were flowers all summer long
in my side pasture, anemones & poppies,
all the largesse of a place
tended a while.

I buy them
when I see them on the street
in tin buckets from those rough men,
the flower men.

There is so much black
I hadn't seen before
in their fast bloom,
at the base of their brilliant throats.

When I stop, stock still,
fishing out my change,
rooting for the coin to keep their impatience
within bounds,

I catch my breath
in the iron music of the steeet;
and feel like a fossil
in a burning museum.

—Margo Lockwood

WHITE SUMMER FLOWER

Nameless

white poppy
whoever looks at you is alone

when I look at your petals
each time they open

and think of each time
that I have passed them

I know that I have wanted
to say Wait

and why should they

—*W. S. Merwin*

ODE TO A DEAD DODGE

Now corn pushes past the foam
rubber front seat where it sprouted,
pale and aiming like a drunk for the light
up front where glass and guessing
became concrete. One ear taps
code on a dud horn.

The corn drives on, gunning 'til fall
the engine, which, as it now stands,
is a sumac, V crotch in the stem,
four-barrelled leaves doing the job
while all around hang those red fuzzy
berries. Very good, I've heard, for tea.

—*David McElroy*

PACKARD

Once, new, you rolled easy and maroon
down a dry Arizona highway.

Somehow, like me, you came to Oregon. Picking up
a couple of coats of cream enamel along the way. I
too have turned a lighter shade.

That was when someone still cared enough
to fix a bashed fender and lead in a dented trunk.
But you moved to the deep woods and
fell on hard times.

I shall not rub salt in fresh wounds
telling sad stories of the sea air. Unwanted, you were
hauled by trailor from the coast to Salem
to turn over a quick buck.

But I, like some silly old lover, have
plucked the rotted cotton from your springs. I
bear you tender gifts of fiberglass, Rustoleum,
WD-40. I shall patch you up and make you anew,
my darling.

Together we shall travel very far indeed.

—*David Barker*

BUICK

As a sloop with a sweep of immaculate wing on her delicate spine
And a keel as steel as a root that holds in the sea as she leans,
Leaning and laughing, my warm-hearted beauty, you ride, you ride,
You tack on the curves with parabola speed and a kiss of goodbye,
Like a thoroughbred sloop, my new high-spirit, my kiss.

As my foot suggests that you leap in the air with your hips of a girl,
My finger that praises your wheel and announced your voices of song,
Flouncing your skirts, you blueness of joy, you flirt of politeness,
You leap, you intelligence, essence of wheelness with silvery nose,
And your platinum clocks of excitement stir like the hairs of a fern.

But how alien you are from the booming belts of your birth and the smoke
Where you turned on the stinging lathes of Detroit and Lansing at night
And shrieked at the torch in your secret parts and the amorous tests,

But now with your eyes that enter the future of roads
you forget;
You are all instinct with your phosphorous glow and
your streaking hair.

And now when we stop it is not as the bird from the
shell that I leave
Or the leathery pilot who steps from his bird with a
sneer of delight,
And not as the ignorant beast do you squat and watch
me depart,
But with exquisite breathing you smile, with satisfac-
tion of love,
And I touch you again as you tick in the silence and
settle in sleep.

—*Karl Shapiro*

CATS

Cats walk neatly
Whatever they pick
To walk upon

Clipped lawn, cool
Stone, waxed floor
Or delicate dust

On feather snow
With what disdain
Lifting a paw

On horizontal glass
No less or
Ice nicely debatable

Wall-to-wall
Carpet, plush divan
Or picket fence

In deep jungle
Grass where we
Can't see them

Where we can't
Often follow follow
Cats walk neatly.

—Robert Francis

THE SECRET IN THE CAT

I took my cat apart
to see what made him purr.
Like an electric clock
or like the snore

of a warming kettle,
something fizzed and sizzled in him.
Was he a soft car,
the engine bubbling sound?

Was there a wire beneath his fur,
or humming throttle?
I undid his throat.
Within was no stir.

I opened up his chest
as though it were a door:
no whisk or rattle there.
I lifted off his skull:

no hiss or murmur.
I halved his little belly
but found no gear,
no cause for static.

So I replaced his lid,
laced his little gut.
His heart into his vest I slid
and buttoned up his throat.

His tail rose to a rod
and beckoned to the air.
Some voltage made him vibrate
warmer than before.

Whiskers and a tail:
perhaps they caught
some radar code
emitted as a pip, a dot-and-dash

of woolen sound.
My cat a kind of tuning fork?—
amplifier?—telegraph?—
doing secret signal work?

His eyes elliptic tubes:
there's a message in his stare.
I stroke him
but cannot find the dial.

—May Swenson

THE KITTEN

The trouble with a kitten is
THAT
Eventually it becomes a
CAT.

—Ogden Nash

CAT ON COUCH

My cat, washing her tail's tip, is a whorl
Of white shell,
As perfect as a fan
In full half-moon . . . Next moment she's a hare:
The muzzle twitches, blurs, goes dumb, and one
Tall ear dips, falters forward . . . Then,
Cross as switches, she's a great horned owl;
Two leafy tricornered ears reverse, a frown
Darkens her chalky visage, big eyes round
And round and stare down midnight.
There sits my cat
Mysterious as gauze,—now somnolent,
Now jocose, quicksilver from a dropped
Thermometer. When poised
Below the sketched ballet-
Dancers who pirouette upon the wall,
Calmly she lifts the slim
Boom of her leg, what will
The prima ballerina next
Perform?—Grace held in readiness.
She meditates, a vision of repose.

—*Barbara Howes*

ACCOMPLISHMENTS

I painted a picture—green sky—and showed it to my
mother.
She said that's nice, I guess.
So I painted another holding the paintbrush in my
teeth,
Look, Ma, no hands. And she said
I guess someone would admire that if they knew
How you did it and they were interested in painting
which I am not.

I played clarinet solo in Gounod's Clarinet Concerto
With the Buffalo Philharmonic. Mother came to listen
and said
That's nice, I guess.
So I played it with the Boston Symphony,
Lying on my back and using my toes,
Look, Ma, no hands. And she said
I guess someone would admire that if they knew
How you did it and they were interested in music
which I am not.

I made an almond souffle and served it to my mother.
She said, that's nice, I guess.
So I made another, beating it with my breath,
Serving it with my elbows,
Look, Ma, no hands. And she said
I guess someone would admire that if they knew
How you did it and they were interested in eating
which I am not.

So I sterilized my wrists, performed the amputation, threw away
My hands and went to my mother, but before I could say
Look, Ma, no hands, she said
I have a present for you and insisted I try on
The blue kid gloves to make sure they were the right size.

—*Cynthia MacDonald*

BARBIE DOLL

This girlchild was born as usual
and presented dolls that did pee-pee
and miniature GE stoves and irons
and wee lipsticks the color of cherry candy.
Then in the magic of puberty, a classmate said:
You have a great big nose and fat legs.

She was healthy, tested intelligent,
possessed strong arms and back,
abundant sexual drive and manual dexterity.
She went to and fro apologizing.
Everyone saw a fat nose on thick legs.

She was advised to play coy,
exhorted to come on hearty,
exercise, diet, smile and wheedle.
Her good nature wore out
like a fan belt.
So she cut off her nose and her legs
and offered them up.

In the casket displayed on satin she lay
with the undertaker's cosmetics painted on,
a turned-up putty nose,
dressed in a pink and white nightie.
Doesn't she look pretty? everyone said.
Consummation at last.
To every woman a happy ending.

—Marge Piercy

&

STRAWBERRIES

The first time I went to the fields alone
I didn't see the strawberries until
I tripped and fell and lay completely still.
Then they came out. One by one at first,
Then clumped in constellations they emerged,
A galaxy of trembling, rooted stars.

But when I picked one and brought it back to earth,
My breathing on it moved it like a wind,
And it turned over in my giant hand
So sure of what it was that it could
Seem to be the accidental meeting
Of three glowing, polished drops of blood.

Berry, berries crushed against my tongue,
Broke the seal on a longing for sweetness
I didn't know was hidden in me.
I ate, reached out and ate. Chords of scent rose
From green, folded hay, my rolling body
And the red stains ripening on my clothes.

I whispered secrets to myself. I felt
The earth tip and the afternoon slide
Toward the edge as I stood up. So I ran
To the dark, inside place called home to bless
Beds and tables with my sweet, red hands.
But they told me I had ruined my dress.

—Judith Hemschemeyer

DOUBLE FEATURE

With Buck still tied to the log, on comes the light.
Lovers disengage, move sheepishly toward the aisle
With mothers, sleep-heavy children, stale perfume, past
 the manager's smile
Out through the velvety chains to the cool air of night.

I dawdle with groups near the rickety pop-corn stand;
Dally at shop windows, still reluctant to go;
I teeter, heels hooked on the curb, scrape a toe;
Or send off a car with vague lifts of a hand.

A wave of Time hangs motionless on this particular
 shore.
I notice a tree, arsenical grey in the light, or the slow
Wheel of the stars, the Great Bear glittering
 colder than snow,
And remember there was something else I was hoping
 for.

—*Theodore Roethke*

BIJOU

Huge, perfect creatures move across the screen
to the rhythms of hidden bands.

Small, imperfect creatures slouch in plush seats
and pull crystal tears from their eyes
when the intellectual dog is lost
or when the nearly nice supporting player
is culled from the action by a villain arrow
while saving the blond-souled hero.
They drop their tears and look around hopefully
when they hear the bugle of a rescue party.
But the aisles are empty. Odorless horses
spring onto the screen below waving flags.

—*Vern Rutsala*

THE POET'S FAREWELL TO HIS TEETH

Now you are going, what can I do but wish you
(as my wife used to say) "every success
in your chosen field."

What we have seen together! Doctor X,
having gagged us, hurling his forceps to the floor
and denouncing our adolescent politics,

or the time we had caught trench-mouth in Iowa City
and had to drive west slowly and haltingly,
spitting in all the branches of the Missouri.

Cigar-stained and tired of cavities, you leave.
It is time to go back to the pure world of teeth
and rest, and compose yourselves for the last eruption.

As to those things in a glass by the bathroom sink
they will never communicate with me as you have done,
fragile and paranoid, sensing the world around you

as wild drills and destructive caramel, getting even
for neglect by waking me into the pain of dawn,
that empty and intimate world of our bitter sharing.

Go, under that cool light. I will remember you:
the paper reports that people may still feel pain
in their missing teeth, as with any amputation.

I hope you relax by the shadowy root canals,
and thinking of me with kindness, but not regret,
toast me just once in the local anaesthetic.

—*William Dickey*

&

MY TEETH

The up-front ones are marvelous,
tiny dancers braving the wind,
shapely and disciplined.

But behind them, corruption,
molars who have lived riotously,
roots eaten by secret lusts
as their bodies disintegrate.
Even the bicuspids and incisors
are infected,
blood swollen
around stiff afflictions of plaque.

The stains of drugs and nicotine
have reached behind the skirts of the dancers,
and it is only a matter of time
before the curtain comes down for good
and the closed mouth
fosters a strange revolution,
the muffled tongue rising
like a brutalized peasantry
to taste its own power
at last.

—Ed Ochester

AFTER THE DENTIST

My left upper
lip and half

my nose is gone.
I drink my coffee

on the right from
a warped cup

whose left lip dips.
My cigarette's

thick as a finger.
Somebody else's.

I put lip-
stick on a cloth-

stuffed doll's
face that's

surprised when one
side smiles.

—*May Swenson*

&

THE ROOT CANAL

You see before you an icing of skin,
a scum of flesh
narrowly wrapped around a tooth.
This too is red as a lion's
heart and it throbs.

This tooth is hollowed out to a cave
big enough for tourists
to go through in parties with guides
in flat-bottomed boats.
This tooth sings opera all night
like a Russian basso profundo.
This tooth plays itself like an organ
in an old movie palace; it is
the chief villain, Sidney Greenstreet,
and its laughter tickles with menace.
This tooth is dying, dying
like a cruel pharoah, like a
fat gouty old tyrant assembling
his wives and his cabinet, his horse
and his generals, his dancing girls
and his hunting cheetah, all
to be burned on his tomb
in homage. I am nothing,
nothing at all, but a reluctant
pyramid standing here, a grandiose
talking headstone for my tooth.

—*Marge Piercy*

CROWS

So. Nine crows to this April field.
Eight grounded dark in a small depression,
the bluets out but the field not green.

Their beaks jutted to feed, the three
to the North are watched by a fourth: he's
on one leg, equally hungry and equally

black, his slack beak heavily open.
The strut of all eight is high, the pasture's
limp; a central three jaunt caucus'd

among the new bluets, talking crow
with no thought of eating. Eight
is on guard, his old beak violent:

he's sighted their ninth, stalled in
from the South, wings down, beak clamped
on bleeding. This much turns out all right:

he's known. And knows where fir carrion
lies, bleached on the road by April sun.
So. April. The crows in possession.

—*Philip Booth*

&

NIGHT CROW

When I saw that clumsy crow
Flap from a wasted tree,
A shape in the mind rose up:
Over the gulfs of dream
Flew a tremendous bird
Further and further away
Into a moonless black,
Deep in the brain, far back.

—*Theodore Roethke*

FROM A BIRCH

from a birch
a crow calls
cracking a morning
dulled by fog

—*P. Wolny*

CROWS

Like the shore's alternation of door   wave
Shoe   wave, the displaced and disturbed
Air replaces itself with more air as casually
As attention grants itself, and I observe
Two crows sew themselves onto the lace flag
Of that flying cloud, whose cosmetic grace
Adorning the Plain Jane face of the day
Pins them in an unlikely halo of pale light
After one blast of which they dance away,
Croaking shrilly as abandoned divas
Whose black scarves flap in the breeze
Over every home and panorama, dark precise
Signs washed up on the air to be noticed
Out of a continuous process of succession

—Tom Clark

THE POET

i beg my bones to be good but
they keep clicking music and
i spin in the center of myself

a foolish frightful woman
moving my skin against the wind and
tap dancing for my life

—Lucille Clifton

&

POET

At his right hand
silence;
at his left hand
silence;
ahead of him
the yahrzeit glass;
behind him
silence;
and above his head
all the letters of the alphabet
to choose from.

—Linda Pastan

REPLY TO THE QUESTION:
"How Can You Become A Poet?"

take the leaf of a tree
trace its exact shape
the outside edges
and inner lines

memorize the way it is fastened to the twig
(and how the twig arches from the branch)
how it springs forth in April
how it is panoplied in July

by late August
crumple it in your hand
so that you smell its end-of-summer sadness

chew its woody stem

listen to its autumn rattle

watch as it atomizes in the November air

then in winter
where there is no leaf left

invent one

—Eve Merriam

I SHOW THE DAFFODILS TO THE RETARDED KIDS

I don't make them name it
like I did with the wooden pig and horse
and the rest in the "animal unit."
I don't even name it myself, or if I do
I don't say it distinctly
with the message, remember!
I take them by the hand and say
I want to show you
something.
When we get to the school steps,
I arrange them around the beds.
Stacy laughs
and opens her palms in a little dance.
I bend down and show them
how to smell: I half close my eyes,
draw my breath in deep,
and look dreamy and delighted. Latasha
pulls a pistil out. David
scolds a whole bed of them with his finger.
Robby bends down with me
and caresses a petal. He gives it a kiss
and one more pat
then he puts the yellow horn to his ear
and listens.

—*Constance Sharp*

CHILDREN NOT KEPT AT HOME

a mile down the road from us
    hidden from the road
there are children not kept at home

some of them bald
    their fin-like structures
hesitant as petals, the delicate

light of their eyes
    unsavage and mild
their faces masks of flesh

the Institution is not bricked up
    the children seem never to approach
the barred windows

in high-chairs they are kingly, queenly—
    saliva flies
their lives fly with the day,
    even

here behind the scabby vines
    even here their lives rise
with the day to ponder eternal souls

unable to walk
    some of them unable to speak or hear
legless or neckless beings yet eternal

a mile down the road in their special home
    unlived lives live
mildly for centuries

—Joyce Carol Oates

&

MY DIM-WIT COUSIN

My dim-wit cousin, saved by a death-bed quaver,
Your little manhood long ago was smothered.
But for an uncle you were thought to favor,
Those doting aunties never would have bothered.

The cost of folly is forever mounting;
Your bed collapses from imagined sins.
Deterioration's scrupulous accounting
Adds up a pair of jiggling double chins.

Your palm is moist, your manner far too jolly . . .
Today, while scraping hair before the mirror,
My shaving hand jerked back in sudden terror:
I heard your laughter rumble from my belly.

—Theodore Roethke

THE CHILDREN

Hand in hand, they are marching
along the hallway, looking
for cats and seagulls,
the footprints of the troll,
speaking to rocks
of a new home for angels,
herding butterflies
in far mountain meadows,
teaching skyscrapers how to swim.

And they are watching,
always, like a row of turtles
on a river bank.
Their eyes look out
from deep within their shells,
where we cannot
see them.

—*Mark Vinz*

THE CHILD IN THE RUG

Better a bug in the dust underfoot
than a human child without a voice.

So when visitors came to her room
she rolled herself in a rug,
lay on the floor and listened.

Fear of the closeness of strangers,
of a word driven deep in her dumbness,
sent her to grieve in a tunnel,

and to think she was all right there,
that she needed no more than this:
to listen to others
through a wall of string,

safe with her moths and pins,
threads of the flowerprints
coming loose from her sky of wool.

—John Haines

THE WINDOWS

Here is a child who presses his head to the ground
his eyes are open
he sees through the window
the flat gray ocean
upside down
with an arbor of islands hanging from it
all the way to the horizon

and he himself is hanging from nothing
he might step down
and walk on the old sky far down there
out to the clouds
in the far islands
he might step on the clouds where they have worn shiny
he might jump from cloud to cloud
he watches lights flash
on and off along the dark shores
and the lights moving among the overhead islands
he feels his head like a boat on a beach
he hears the waves break around his ears
he stands up and listens
he turns to a room full of his elders
and the lights on
blue day in the far empty windows
and without moving he flies

—*W. S. Merwin*

OLD MEN

People expect old men to die,
They do not really mourn old men.
Old men are different. People look
At them with eyes that wonder when . . .

People watch with unshocked eyes;
But the old men know when an old man dies.

—*Ogden Nash*

&

THE TWO OLD GENTLEMEN

Though the house had burned years ago,
with everything in it,
all that had been brought out in the wagons,
all that had been added since,
the photographs, the pink-flowered paper,
the stuffed furniture from St. Louis,
the blue gilt set of Dickens their father
had ordered from the salesman out from St. Louis—

Though the house had burned years ago,
they always talked of it
and of the times there had been in it
when they were boys, before they were boys,
the uncle who had been wounded at Antietam
and had come west and died before they were born,
their mother churning on the porch, the arrowheads
they once found along the banks of the green creek—

Though the house had burned years ago,
with everything in it,
they sat talking, these childless gentlemen,
in the sun-high field where the hay was making,
these gentle children by the big red baler,
talking of Mr. Micawber and Little Nell,
of Dombey, and Krook who turned to smoke,
and Pickwick travelling the road to Norwich.

—Robert Wallace

&

THE OLD MEN

The fish has too many bones
and the watermelon too many seeds.

—Charles Reznikoff

WAR STORY

Of one who grew up at Gallipoli
Not over months and miles, but in the space
Of feet and half a minute. Wading shoreward
With a plague of bullets pocking the sea

He tripped, as it seemed to him over his scabbard,
And stubbed his fingers on a dead man's face.

—*John Stallworthy*

&

A WAR

There set out, slowly, for a Different World.
At four, on winter mornings, different legs . . .
You can't break eggs without making an omelette
—That's what they tell the eggs.

—*Randall Jarrell*

&

A POST-MORTEM

Searching for souvenirs among some rubble,
A post-atomic-warfare man observed
That "those who made this little bit of trouble
Got only what they asked for and deserved."
    Then, in a kindlier afterthought's release,
    He pitied "them that only asked for peace."

—*Siegfried Sassoon*

&

RADAR

Distance is swept by the smooth
Rotations of power, whose staring
Feelers multiply our eyes for us,
Mark objects' range and bearing.

Linked to them, guns rehearse
Calculated obedience; echoes of light
Trigger the shadowing needle, determine
The flaring arrest of night.

Control is remote: feelings, like hands,
Gloved by space. Responsibility is shared, too:
And destroying the enemy by radar,
We cannot see what we do.

—*Alan Ross*

THE GLUTTON

The jowls of his belly crawl and swell like the sea
When his mandibles oily with lust champ and go wide;
Eternal, the springs of his spittle leak at the lips
Suspending the tongue like a whale that rolls on the
tide.

His hands are as rotten fruit. His feet are as corn.
Deep are the wells of his eyes and like navels, blind.
Dough is the brain that supplies his passion with bread.
Dough is the loose-slung sack of his great behind.

Will his paps become woman's? He dreams of the yielding of milk,
Despising the waste of his stool that recalls him to bread;
More than passion of sex and the transverse pains of disease
He thinks of starvation, the locked-up mouth of the dead.

I am glad that his stomach will eat him away in revenge,
Digesting itself when his blubber is lain in the earth.
Let the juice of his gluttony swallow him inward like lime
And leave of his volume only the mould of his girth.

—Karl Shapiro

&

THE FAT MAN

I call everyone
shriveled. Dried apples
fit for cellars,
nothing more.

They have no folds,
no flesh to touch—
gangling reminders
of the grave.

Existence melts
in my mouth.
I relish, I taste
the sweet jams of life;
I gorge and worship
the place of love:
all kitchens everywhere.

Diet is sin:
an effort
to turn limbs
to razors that slice
a lover's hand.
Right angles
pierce my eye;
I love the arc,
soft oval, the curve—
things molded
to be touched,
the soothers of sight.

I feel at least
ten souls
swimming in my flesh.
I feed them
with both hands.

Someday
I will become
a mountain.
I eat the world.

—Vern Rutsala

THE AMPUTATION

More than he mourned for walking he grieved
   for the presence
of the leg, and more than for the dancing
   he hadn't, for all
his nineteen years, done much of yet. It became to him
Like a lost lover, all things because all lost—
   the diamond
part of his self, fleshed like roses.
   He cried in the night
for its substance, and felt it there! there! there!
Felt it itch, felt the complexity of its ankle,
   the satiny
socket; the authority of its heel;
   moved its toes and had to
touch the sudden stump in the darkest of darknesses
   to know the truth.

Sometimes in dreams he had it back, the sunrise grass
wet
and prickly under his bare feet. The leg was his friend,
his companion. He stitched it in place in dreams,
had it tattooed with his name. He balanced his big
blond
weight on it and spun like a dervish. The joy of that!

Waking, loss engulfed him. Waking again and again,
grief
burned him thin and hard. The leg lay still in its grave
and he acknowledged the grave at last. He learned to
walk
on a stubborn, bloodless copy of his severed limb.
And not to think of it any more.

—Helen Sorrells

THE LEG

Among the iodoform, in twilight-sleep,
What have I lost? he first inquires,
Peers in the middle distances where a pain,
Ghost of a nurse, hazily-moves, and day,
Her blinding presence pressing in his eyes
And now his tears. They are handling him
With rubber gloves. He wants to get up.

One day beside some flowers near his nose
He will be thinking, *When will I look at it?*
And pain, still in the middle distance, will reply,
At what? and he will know it's gone,
O where! and begin to tremble and cry.
He will begin to cry as a child cries
Whose puppy is mangled under a screaming wheel.

Later, as if deliberately, his fingers
Begin to explore the stump. He learns a shape
That is comfortable and tucked in like a sock.
This has a sense of humor, this can despise
The finest surgical limb, the dignity of limping,
The nonsense of wheel-chairs. Now he smiles to the
 wall:
The amputation becomes an acquisition.

For the leg is wondering where he is
 (all is not lost)
And surely he has a duty to the leg;
He is its injury, the leg is his orphan,
He must cultivate the mind of the leg,
Pray for the part that is missing, pray for peace
In the image of man, pray, pray for its safety,
And after a little it will die quietly.

The body, what is it, Father, but a sign
To love the force that grows us, to give back
What in Thy palm is senselessness and mud?
Knead, knead the substance of our understanding
Which must be beautiful in flesh to walk,
That if Thou take me angrily in hand
And hurl me to the shark, I shall not die!

—*Karl Shapiro*

ON A CHILD WHO LIVED ONE MINUTE

Into a world where children shriek like suns
sundered from other suns on their arrival,
she stared, and saw the waiting shape of evil,
but could not take its meaning in at once,
so fresh her understanding, and so fragile.

Her first breath drew a fragrance from the air
and put it back. However hard her agile
heart danced, however full the surgeon's satchel
of healing stuff, a blackness tiptoed in her
and snuffed the only candle of her candle.

Oh, let us do away with elegiac
drivel! Who can restore a thing so brittle,
so new in any jingle? Still I marvel
that, making light of mountainloads of logic,
so much could stay a moment in so little.

—X. J. Kennedy

&

TO EVAN

I wanted to give him some gift,
The breath of my breath, the look of my eyes,
I wanted to give him some gift,
Lying there so piteously.

I wanted to give him some gift,
Small child dying slowly,
With brave blue intelligent eyes,
His form withered piteously.

Only in the intelligence of those eyes
Where life had retreated for a piercing look
Was the enormous mystery justified,
As he inhaled the betraying oxygen.

I wanted to give him some gift,
A look from my look not to frighten him,
A breath from my haleness, my even vigor,
The same breath as his lonely breath.

Tenacious life in this little form
That will soon vanish from it entirely,
Unforgettable features of this little boy,
Do you mock my passion in your long passing?

I wanted to give him some gift,
Breath of my breath, the look of my eyes,
This is all upon earth, under heaven
I can give him, a child dying, and I unwise.

Though I would menace the tall skies
And cry out as man has from the beginning
At the unequal fate held over us from our birth
I could not for a moment suspend this child's dying.

O though I would look into his intelligent eyes
With the world's weight of experience and despair
I could not mate the black look before death,
Nor seize the secret from the secrecy.

I wanted to give him some gift,
Breath of my breath, the look of my eyes.
Farewell, fair spirit. Fare forward, voyager.
I pass away silently and see him no more.

—Richard Eberhart

ANTHONY

Your absent name at rollcall was more present
than you ever were, forever
on parole in the back of the class.
The first morning you were gone,
we practiced penmanship to keep our minds
off you. My first
uncoiled chains of connecting circles,
oscilloscopic hills;
my carved-up desk, rippled as a washboard.

A train cut you in half in the Jersey marshes.
You played there after school.
I thought of you and felt afraid.
One awkward *a* multiplied into a fence
running across the page.
I copied out two rows of *b*'s.
The caboose of the last *d* ran smack against
the margin. Nobody even liked you!
My *e*'s and *f*'s travelled over the snowy landscape
on parallel tracks—the blue guidelines
that kept our letters even.

The magician sawed his wife in half.
He passed his hand through the gulf of air
where her waist should be.
Divided into two boxes, she turned and smiled
and all her ten toes flexed.
I skipped a line.

I dotted the disconnected body of each *i.*
At the bottom of the page,
I wrote your name. Erased it.
Wrote it, and erased again.

—Jane Shore

MOVING

Some of the sky is grey and some of it is white.
The leaves have lost their heads
And are dancing round the tree in circles, dead;
The cat is in it.
A smeared, banged, tow-headed
Girl in a flowered, flour-sack print
Sniffles and holds up her last bite
Of bread and butter and brown sugar to the wind.

Butter the cat's paws
And bread the wind. We are moving.
I shall never again sing
Good morning, Dear Teacher, to my own dear teacher.
Never again
Will Augusta be the capital of Maine.

The dew has rusted the catch of the strap of my satchel
And the sun has fallen from the place where it was
  chained
With a blue construction-paper chain . . .
Someone else must draw the bow
And the blunderbuss, the great gobbler
Upside-down under the stone arrow
In the black, bell-brimmed hat—
And the cattycornered bat.
The witch on the blackboard
Says: "Put the Plough into the Wagon
Before it turns into a Bear and sleeps all winter
In your play-house under the catalpa."
Never again will Orion
Fall on my speller through the star
Taped on the broken window by my cot.
My knee is ridged like corn
And the scab peels off it.

We are going to live in a new pumpkin
Under a gold star.

There is not much else.
The wind blows somewhere else.
The brass bed bobs to the van.
The broody hen
Squawks upside-down—her eggs are boiled;
The cat is dragged from the limb.
The little girl
Looks over the shoulders of the moving-men
At her own street;

And, yard by lot, it changes.
Never again.
But she feels her tea-set with her elbows
And inches closer to her mother;
Then she shuts her eyes, and sits there, and squashed
  red
Circles and leaves like colored chalk
Come on in her dark head
And are darkened, and float farther
And farther and farther from the stretched-out hands
That float out from her in her broody trance:
She hears her own heart and her cat's heart beating.

She holds the cat so close to her he pants.

—Randall Jarrell

GOING AWAY

Now as the year turns toward its darkness
the car is packed, and time come to start
driving west. We have lived here
for many years and been more or less content;
now we are going away. That is how
things happen, and how into new places,
among other people, we shall carry
our lives with their peculiar memories
both happy and unhappy but either way

touched with the strange tonality
of what is gone but inalienable, the clear
and level light of a late afternoon
out on the terrace, looking to the mountains,
drinking with friends. Voices and laughter
lifted in still air, in a light
that seemed to paralyze time.
We have had kindness here, and some
unkindness; now we are going on.
Though we are young enough still
and militant enough to be resolved,
keeping our faces to the front, there is
a moment, after saying all farewells,
when we taste the dry and bitter dust
of everything that we have said and done
for many years, and our mouths are dumb,
and the easy tears will not do. Soon
the north wind will shake the leaves,
the leaves will fall. It may be
never again that we shall see them,
the strangers who stand on the steps,
smiling and waving, before the screen doors
of their suddenly forbidden houses.

—*Howard Nemerov*

&

MOVING IN WINTER

Their life, collapsed like unplayed cards,
is carried piecemeal through the snow:
headboard and footboard now, the bed
where she has lain desiring him
where overhead his sleep will build
its canopy to smother her once more;
their table, by four elbows worn
evening after evening while the wax runs down;
mirrors grey with reflecting them,
bureaus coffining from the cold
things that can shuffle in a drawer,
carpets rolled up around those echoes
which, shaken out, take wing and breed
new altercations, the old silences.

—Adrienne Rich

YUGOSLAV CEMETERY
Jackson, California

At Gettysburg full anonymity:
Number for him whose name is past recall;
The marker dwindles, and the turf appears
Scant for a soldier's wear. (Can this be all?)

But here each granite bears a photograph:
As from a window, personality—
A miniature wraith—is gazing out,
Rain on the cheek in wistful parody.

Slavic inscriptions cannot hide this pair,
Wholly themselves, too young for such a bed;
Miner who died of silicosis; wife
thin-faced and dark, with braids about her head.

Quietly as their neighbors they persist,
Preserve their essence, hint their special pain;
We are intruding on their privacy,
These large-eyed mournful lovers in the rain.

—*Celeste Turner Wright*

A CITY GRAVEYARD

Beyond the iron-barred fence
traffic moves quick
as the eyes of squirrels
treed in this block-sized park
of the dead
tidy and dried are the geraniums in their beds
heavy the odd stocky benches of wood and concrete

here, children cut through the graveyard
bound for home
cut-outs of pumpkins in orange and crude crayons,
   fluttering
quicker
than the leftover
flowers
the tassels of artificial bouquets
the children's voices are unguarded

banked gently as the beds of bedrooms
are the graves' inclines
and the gravestones have the cautious empty stare
of civilized people
as people who are visitors here
walk slowly through the aisles
studious, reverent before the Latin words
the names and prophecies
personality gone impersonal

from the boulevard the unserious sighs of exhaust
from the children needle-thin shrieks
the dead have many powers
deadly their piled-up bodies, their powdered weights
deadly their incantations carved in stone
their fingers grasping blade-like, grassy at our ankles

if we touch each other by accident here
we recoil
our fingers fear intimacy, here
our eyes, here, slant away from one another
the dead have no power except their weight
their drain upon our gravity
our small tireless names
murmured in their voices.

—Joyce Carol Oates

IN A COUNTRY CEMETERY IN IOWA
for James Hearst

Someone's been up here nights,
and in a hurry,
breaking the headstones.

And someone else,
with a little time to spare,
has mended them;

some farmer, I'd say,
who knows his welding.
He's stacked them up in

harnesses of iron,
old-angle-iron and strap,
taking a little extra time

to file the welds down smooth.
Just passing through, you'd say
it looks like foolishness.

—Ted Kooser

YOUTH

is the ability to be
single-minded as water caressing a stone
and ambidextrous as the wind
ringing all its bells
at the same time

but tomorrow is over
so what can I do with today
coming as it does at the wrong time
for everybody including me

who wasted my youth in celibacy
hard work and studies
and now find myself
turning to riotous living in vain

what does the water feel
just as it gets to the edge and decides
to go down
what does the wind have to say
about the direction it is blowing

we do not choose what we must have
but we must have it anyway
and if we cannot get it
we will die

I do not know what happens after that
to our transparent lives
or to the wreckage
our lack of dreams creates

when I tell the truth
there is so little to say

—Richard Shelton

&

BOY AT A CERTAIN AGE

Perfectly rounded yet how slender
Supple, pliable, puppy-limber
Whole body lifts to lift a finger.

A mouth efficient for drinking, eating
Just as sufficient for shouting, beeping
But not yet for connected speaking.

A voice combining bass and treble
A mind more dreamable than thinkable
From chin to toe smooth as a pebble.

—*Robert Francis*

&

PORTRAIT OF THE BOY AS ARTIST

Were he composer, he would surely write
A quartet for three orchestras, one train:
After the penny-whistle's turn, he might—
With ten bull-fiddles purring the refrain—
Dub in a lion to outroar the night.

Were he a painter, he would loose such bolts
Of color as would scare the sun, abash
Rainbows: a palomino-coated colt
Gallops on every speckled plain: a gashed
Knee bleeds rubies: frogs are emerald.

Were he a poet with the gift of tongues,
He'd scale the Andes in a metaphor.
Race Theseus in the labyrinth, among
Larks and angels act as troubadour,
For Daniel Boone shout at the top of his lungs.

Clear-eyed he sallies forth upon the field,
Holding close to his ear the shell of the world.

—Barbara Howes

WONDERS OF THE WORLD

light is a vehicle for shadows
darkness brings only itself

mountains and continents
rising falling
the earth breathes slowly

the river always moving on
the sea always trying to get out

it is cold and they are naked
but the trees catch snow
in their hands

the rain in all its moods
still anonymous

the star in the apple
the nest in the pomegranate
the maze in the onion

—Richard Shelton

THE GIFT

One day
as I was lying on the lawn
dreaming of the Beautiful
and my wife was justifiably bitching
  out the window
at my shiftlessness and
the baby was screaming
because I wouldn't let him
eat my cigarettes,
a tiger cat leaped over the fence,
smiled at my wife,
let the baby pull his tail,
hummed like a furry dynamo
as I stroked him.

My wife took the car to get some food,
my son began to sing his wordless song,
and I wrote a poem in the sand.

Now God give every man who's hopeless
a beautiful wife,
an infant son who sings,
and the gift of a sweet-faced cat.

—*Ed Ochester*

&

WALKING IN THE RAIN

walking in the rain
the earth has more than
four corners
the earth is a saucer
upside down
i reach for the stars
and pass my arms
through a cloud
i rise off my feet
and hold the moon
against my chest
i caress it and move on
the sun is soon beneath me
and i pick it up and put my
arm through it, and it is a
ring about my muscle
soon i wear it as a wreath
around my neck and smile.

—*Dan Saxon*

&

LINES FOR A FRIEND WHO LEFT

"Ich starre, wie des Steins Inneres starrat."
—R. M. Rilke

Something vague waxes or wanes.
I have been grieving since you've gone,
and I am stark as the heart of the stone.
I have this grief because you are a ghost
and a thief. Since you left I have missed
my own self. For your absence
steals my presence.
Next I lost my dignity. At night
I put on the dirty shirt
and coat you left
and go out
to hunt for you in the bar or street
feeling your private warmth. Last night
I thought I saw your very face
(voice of another)
in the place of a folk singer.
(The heavy mouth almost seemed to sneer
at the end. I could not be sure.)
I have not heard
since you've gone, so I still yearn
for any sign
of your life. For if you died
I did too. I

Can no longer quite
make out your body's breadth and height,
and there is something vague that grows in me
like a dead child.
Write
or come back, before I forget
what we both look like.

—John Logan

POEM

I loved my friend.
He went away from me.
There's nothing more to say.
The poem ends,
Soft as it began—
I loved my friend.

—Langston Hughes

THE ARRIVAL OF MY MOTHER
–New Mexico, 1906

She got off, according to the diary,
dressed in a lovely beaded gown, fresh
from Washington with sixteen trunks of ball gowns,
chemises, blouses (4 Middie), shoes and assorted
lingerie. She was at that time about 25, old
for an unmarried woman. Her stiff mother was at
her side, she also wildly overdressed for New Mexico
sun and wind.

What must she have thought, seeing my uncle standing
hat in hand in the dust of that lonely train house,
cracked yellow paint, faded letters of welcome
for passengers that rarely come?

The buckboard was waiting and they rode out into
the darkness of evening toward the tent, the half
built frame homestead house, wind dying as the sun
sank, bird cries stilled.

I see her now outshooting my father and me, laughing
at our pride and embarrassment. My sister as good a
shot, waiting her turn. Or that picture of her
on horseback, in Eastern riding clothes beside the
Pecos.
A picnic when I was small and how my father lifted me
up
to her and she carefully walked the horse around rock
and sand.

I suppose she finally arrived in New Mexico
in the April of one year when my sister and I sat beside
a rented bed, each holding one of her hands and
watched
her eyes grow childlike, unmasked as a *kachina*
entering the final *kiva* of this Dance. The graceful
the slim laughing woman of my childhood. The old
mother
heavy with her eyes slipped away and the woods of
New
England dimmed as these dry hills ripened and caught
her last breath, drums, drums should have beaten
for the arrival of my mother.

—*Keith Wilson*

IF THERE ARE ANY HEAVENS

if there are any heavens my mother will (all by herself)
have
one. It will not be a pansy heaven or
a fragile heaven of lilies-of-the-valley but
it will be a heaven of blackred roses

my father will be (deep like a rose
tall like a rose)

standing near my

(swaying over her
silent)
with eyes which are really petals and see

nothing with the face of a poet really which
is a flower and not a face with
hands
which whisper
This is my beloved my
(suddenly in sunlight

he will bow,
and the whole garden will bow)

—e. e. cummings

PORTRAIT OF MY MOTHER ON HER WEDDING DAY

A young woman,
lilies gathered to her breast—
the moment of the wave
before it crests—
bride,
incandescent,
even in this sepia image
dazzling me, like a wedding guest.

Fifty years later, I uncover
in the movement of her swept-back veil
the life that was to come,
seeing revealed
the cunning of those hands
that clasp the flowers;
the will to shape a world
of her devising.

And once again I feel
how evil seems to fall away
before the power of her candid gaze
while everything in us that answers to good,
crowds round her lap
hearing itself spoken of.

—Celia Gilbert

SWIMMER

1.
Observe how he negotiates his way
With trust and the least violence, making
The stranger friend, the enemy ally.
The depth that could destroy gently supports him.
With water he defends himself from water.
Danger he leans on, rests in. The drowning sea
Is all he has between himself and drowning.

2.
What lover ever lay more mutually
With his beloved, his always-reaching arms
Stroking in smooth and powerful caresses?
Some drown in love as in dark water, and some
By love are strongly held as the green sea
Now holds the swimmer. Indolently he turns
To float.—The swimmer floats, the lover sleeps.

—Robert Francis

&

NEAR DROWNING

Loss of weight.
Sensation of other air.
Tightening,
                    sinking,
stiff with fright;

dropping
until the bottom frees you at last
and you retake the surface and its dare.

Then down again,
down,
down,
as if falling was the only direction
your
body   with all your might
knew,   up again
to
push
scaling heights that
vanish as you climb . . .

The waves' white hands
clap for you to stay!

A great lion is gathering to leap.

You leap,
dash,
roll,
shudder onto sand,
and somehow claim it—
holding,
holding
to keep.

—*Ralph Pomeroy*

&

LAMENT FOR THE NON-SWIMMERS

They never feel they can be well in the water,
Can come to rest, that their bodies are light.
When they reach out, their cupped hands hesitate:
What they wanted runs between their fingers.
Their fluttering, scissoring legs sink under.

Their bones believe in heaviness, their ears
Shake out the cold invasion of privacy,
Their eyes squeeze shut. Each breath,
Only half air, is too breath-taking.
The dead-man's float seems strictly for dead men.

They stand in the shallows, their knees touching,
Their feet where they belong in the sand.
They wade as carefully as herons, but hope for nothing
Under the surface, that wilderness
Where eels and sharks slip out of their element.

Those who tread water and call see their blurred eyes
Turn distant, not away from a sky's reflection
As easy to cross as the dependable earth
But from a sight as blue as drowned men's faces.
They splash ashore, pretending to feel buoyant.

—David Wagoner

INSOMNIA

hounds charging from one wall to another
the beating of crazy wings
something at the window
tapping like glass upon glass

sleepless, my eyes have clouded over
I remain myself
there is no descent tonight to the cemetery of sleepers
no mingling of arms and legs
lazily lost in that element

I stare upon the shelf that is me
imprisoned in a box of four stark walls
panic rises sparkling along the legs
feathery behind the knees in that most intimate of
  places

I lie in bed symmetrical as a figure
on a ship's prow or on a tomb
hands folded in the caution of insomnia
the ache of being is everywhere in this room
ache of self like twine tightened around the head

we were born to drown in a blizzard of dreams
and sleepless, we are giant eyes
sleepless, we are protuberances
on the surface of the night
irritating the natural contours of the earth

—*Joyce Carol Oates*

INSOMNIA THE GEM OF THE OCEAN

When I lay me down to sleep
My waterbed says, "Gurgle gleep,"
And when I readjustment crave
It answers with a tidal wave
That lifts me like a bark canoe
Adrift in breakers off Peru.

Neap to my spring, ebb to my flow,
It turns my pulse to undertow,
It turns my thoughts to bubbles, it
Still undulates when I would quit;
Two bags of water, it and I
In restless sympathy here lie.

—*John Updike*

INSOMNIA

Where is that plain door?
That narrow passage,
the hourglass
point where white changes
to soft black: how can
a conscious mind
remember the way through
to embrace its small death?

How beautiful are the waters
of sleep rushing on,
how gratifying is that calm pond
under the fish gape
of the swimming moon.

How full of life the tides
rising and ebbing in every
salty estuary of the flesh,
rich as the sea with neon plankton,
with ancient monsters
sleeking through depths
that flatten and deform
leaching the ordinary colors.

For nine days I have lost my way,
I have been wandering all night
back corridors, drafty, dreary, ill lit
with doors banging and warnings flashing
tedious as aching molars,
as I search the way through.

I am a bulb left
to burn itself out.
What grumpy clatter
of my forebrain buzzing.
With shame I watch my cats.
Sleep is in the benediction
of the body on the brain
at ease, simple
as breathing.

—Marge Piercy

HOUSE-HUNTING

The wind has twisted the roof from an old house
    And thrown it away,
And no one's going to live there anymore.
    It tempts me:
Why not have weather falling in every room?

Isn't the sky
As easy to keep up as any ceiling?
Less flat and steady?
Rain is no heavier, soaking heavy heads,
Than a long party.
Imagine moonlight from a chandelier,
Sun through the laundry,
The snow on conversation, leaves in the bed,
Fog in the library,
Or yourself in a bathtub hoping for the best
As clouds go by,
Dressing for dinner according to what comes down
And not how many.
And at night, to sit indoors would be to lose
Nothing but privacy
As the crossing stars took time to mark their flight
Over the mind's eye.

—*David Wagoner*

ON THE HOUSE OF A FRIEND
(*for Robert Sund*)

Under the lightly leaved
April trees,
your small red house seems to speak—
mildly. It lets you come down
into it from the easy sloping lawn.

Your house is very clean,
for each room
has been well swept by your young friends.
You gave up your bed to them
because they are in love: the lean,
glad girl with long hands
who shares easily all she has
with her blond, gentle boy.
It is this the house seems to say
at the Dutch, open half-door:
their love and yours.
Look, a hapless slug
suns and glows on the madrona stump
beside the porch. So slow, so
slowly it goes
toward the great, full mushroom
resting there. That house
shall keep him from harm.
Beside the rhododendrons in the yard,
your red, Iceland
daisies make a light sound.
Their music seems to change and go
between the flowers and the glass in the window.
Robert, now this small
red house (as in a child's
book) smiles
with the smile of your own face.

—John Logan

&

ANN'S HOUSE

when my house is full of flowers the brightness
is better than sun: when afternoons
are long shadows in the east rooms
violets glow in the near darkness   a red
rose opens like the sound of a lute but
winters they all sleep and wait   white
white are the April beds

—Dick Lourie

THE HOUSE REMEMBERS

Faces, voices, yes of course
and the food eaten and the fires kindled
but the house also remembers feet.

Especially how one big pair used to pad
about comfortable as a cat's
bare on the bare wood floor.

And somebody else in clean white heavy socks
(his boots left at the door) would curl up
tailor-wise, Buddha-wise, on the couch

And only then the talk could really begin
and go on without end while listener
sat opposite and listened.

And once when one big toe had broken bounds
how someone took the sock and darned it
while the wearer sat and wondered.

Blisters to operate on but before
the sterile needle the basin of warm water
and someone kneeling as in the Last Supper.

What fireplace naturally remembers
are the cold feet it warmed but does it
recall the time when fire was not enough

And someone took bare feet in his bare hands
and chafed and cheered the blood
while the fire went on quietly burning?

—Robert Francis

THE GRANDMOTHER

Better born than married, misled,
in the heavy summers of the river bottom
and the long winters cut off by snow
she would crave gentle dainty things,
"a pretty little cookie or a cup of tea,"

but spent her days over a wood stove
cooking cornbread, kettles of jowl and beans
for the heavy, hungry, hard-handed
men she has married and mothered, bent
past unbending by her days of labor
that love had led her to. They had to break her
before she would lie down in her coffin.

—*Wendell Berry*

MY GRANDMOTHER HAD BONES

My grandmother had bones as delicate
As ivory umbrella ribs. Orphaned
Early, she craved things no one could give her.
She boiled kettles dry and threw in her hand
If she was losing. No one outlived her,
But her health was never quite good. Her cat
Killed birds and made her cry. Still she kept him.
She loved green tea, postcards, things from far off.
"Where does the time go to" she would sigh.
She went to bed, to mass, coughed her little cough.
She braided my hair like honey, but I
Had Mother do it over tight. Some whim
Made her dislike me, but I didn't care,
I thought. Why then, when she died, did I dream
She was a package of frozen meat?
Why was I chosen to throw her in the stream?

Why, when I had the bundle gathered neat
Did her raw wristbone scrape against my hair?

—Judith Hemschemeyer

&

GOOSEBERRIES

On his deathbed my grandfather
sang about meeting his wife in heaven.
he, a weaver, who as a young man had
yodelled across the Alps to his sheep,
and on Saturdays wheeled a lawnmower
through town to care for relatives in the cemetery,
spent Saturday nights drinking
a glass of beer with his violin,
at last succumbed, a skeleton
floating in the sea of sheets.
beneath his chin he saw the ribs
opening and through the skin the fine webs
of his hands making their final gestures
past his face. he nodded at the fiery
wolves that snorted around his bed as they had
around the bed of his mother gone crazy. at the last
he remarked our bodies were clothed in heat wavering
in that inland house with its widow's walk
higher than the maples

he went hungering up the chimney
all in one piece, and his little wife
who baked for him ran out
            and tore up the gooseberries.

—Peter Wild

&

GRANDMOTHER

No one remembered when she first discovered God.
Her conversion was sudden as a slammed door.
Outside, my grandfather beat the doorjam with his fist,
But she, God-furious, would not relent.
Shut up like an oyster on a speck of dirt
She praised God in her bedclothes,
Read the Bible like a French novel,
And dreamed each night of Christ the Savior,
The lightning bolt of revelation forking at her
From the black cloud of her Bible,
And the godhead stirring inside her like a sick sea.

Overnight her skirt grew longer and her temper
  shorter,
The black buttons on her boots crept higher and higher
On legs that had never seen the light.
Whenever she rode the cable car downtown
She pulled her bonnet tight around her ears
To let no evil words hiss through,

Her eyes magnified by scripture,
Split by the seeing lens and reading lens
Which could never look together,
Beholders of two worlds: one black and one white,
Negative, censored, and unprintable,
A damned world bleached of color.

Stern as an iron stove
She drove her children off to church,
Beat their bottoms with willow
To make them kneel like thirteen sinful sheep,
Recalcitrant, flagellant, bleating at the altar,
Pinched upright in their pews,
Reciting alphabets of sin while the preacher,
A red-faced Russian with a beard as black as God
Gospeled from the pulpit
And the congregation flapped their tongues,
Prophesying improbable forgiveness.

But nothing ever was:
The family scattered out like rabbits
From the sawed-off shotgun of the true faith
While Grandmother rocked in the cradle of belief,
Reading and praying, reading and praying,
Copying scriptures on tiny scraps of paper
That peeped like mice or children
From every nook and cranny of the old house:
From cookie jars and table drawers and kitchen cup-
  boards—
Even from the Bible itself, marsupial
  with misconceptions,

Threatening every minute to explode,
Until one day her heart did,
And we hunkered in the shadow of her death,
A bad-luck come-to-nothing family
Wrong since genesis.

—Henry Carlile

THE CANARY

The song of canaries
Never varies,
And when they're moulting
They're pretty revolting.

—Ogden Nash

CARDINAL

With deep snow
  A fresh page
    Stretches
    Toward the tree-
  Line; within, a new page
Reflects the grey-white of

Ceiling; never flat,
    Snow rolls with the
        Earth's breathing—
        Slivers
    Of light, reflected,
Skate like grasshoppers

Over the whole white-
    Carpeted landscape,
        Or again, in grey
        Weather, blend into
    Dusk;—those matchstick
Trees out there, poled

Into snow, are characters
    Cutting their own shadow. My
        Page now has markings:
        Hieroglyphs of
    Talon, pen, shade,
Hoof range over this open

Country, imprint it. On snow-
    Fall—as the white
        Magic between us
        Is signed—I see
    The cardinal's red cursive
Line, written on winter, writing to spring . . .

—*Barbara Howes*

&

THE RED-WING BLACKBIRD

The wild red-wing black
bird croaks frog
like though more shrill
as the beads of

his eyes blaze over the
swamp and the o-
dors of the swamp vodka
to his nostrils

—*William Carlos Williams*

BAY BANK

The red-winged blackbird
lighting
dips deep the
windy bayridge
reed but
sends a song up
reed and wind rise to.

—*A. R. Ammons*

GNAT ON MY PAPER

He has two antennae,
They search back and forth,
Left and right, up and down.

He has four feet,
He is exploring what I write now.

This is a living being,
Is this a living poem?

His life is a quarter of an inch.
I could crack him any moment now.

Now I see he had two more feet,
Almost too delicate to examine.

He is still sitting on this paper,
An inch away from An.

Does he know who I am,
Does he know the importance of man?

He does not know or sense me,
His antennae are still sensing.

I wonder if he knows it is June,
The world in its sensual height?

How absurd to think
That he never thought of Plato.

He is satisfied to sit on this paper,
For some reason he has now flown away.

Small creature, gnat on my paper,
Too slight to be given a thought,

I salute you as evanescent,
I play with you in my depth.

What, still here? Still evanescent?
You are my truth, that vanishes.

Now I put down this paper,
He has flown into the infinite.
He could not say it.

—*Richard Eberhart*

INTERLUDE

Writing, I crushed an insect with my nail
And thought nothing at all. A bit of wing
Caught my eye then, a gossamer so frail

And exquisite, I saw in it a thing
That scorned the grossness of the thing I wrote.
It hung upon my finger like a sting.

A leg I noticed next, fine as a mote,
"And on this frail eyelash he walked," I said,
"And climbed and walked like any mountain-goat."

And in this mood I sought the little head
But it was lost; then in my heart a fear
Cried out, "A life—why beautiful, why dead!"

It was a mite that held itself most dear,
So small I could have drowned it with a tear.

—Karl Shapiro

&

TO THE FLY IN MY DRINK

You wouldn't listen to my wordless temperance
  lecture—
    The back of my hand—but hovered
Over my glass, tempted, already groggy, and finally
    Plunged when I wasn't looking,
Were soaked before I could swizzle you out of this low
  dive.
    Your feathery nose for news,
Your magnetic legs, your agile acrobat's wings, and all
    Your myriad eyes have had it.

Here's mud in those eyes. This drink is on you,
    a libation poured
        With genuine regret
In a garden where some cold-sober slug will celebrate
        Your wake through the night.

—David Wagoner

SUNDAY

Up early while everyone sleeps,
I wander through the house,
pondering the eloquence
of vacant furniture, listening
to birdsong peeling
the cover off the day.

I think everyone I know
is sleeping now. Sidewalks
are cool, waiting for
roller skaters and wagons.
Skate keys are covered
with dew; bicycles look
broken, abandoned on the lawns—
no balance left in them,
awkward as wounded
animals. I am the last

man and this is my
last day; I can't think
of anything to do. Somewhere
over my shoulder a jet
explores a crease
in the cloudy sky;
I sit on the porch
waiting for things to happen.

O fat god of Sunday
and chocolate bars, watcher
over picnics and visits to the zoo,
will anyone wake up today?

—Vern Rutsala

SUNDAY RAIN

The window screen
is trying to do
its crossword puzzle
but appears to know
only vertical words.

—John Updike

ON A SUNDAY

On a Sunday, when the place was closed,
I saw a plump mouse among the cakes in the window:
dear ladies,
who crowd this expensive tearoom,
you must not think that you alone are blessed of God.

—*Charles Reznikoff*

SUNDAY FUNNIES

I can remember lying
stretched-out,
backs close against the sagging bed's
worn green spread,
with the Sunday funnies covering our
selves
like a comical umbrella.
He lay between us;
my sister, long and quiet,
piercing brown eyes
taking in all;
me, curls of body and black hair,
turning, wriggling
in anticipation of
Joe Palooka
beyond Dick Tracy's blocked-out smile.

Sheltered in a world of bright colors
and laughing heroes,
my father, wire glasses resting uselessly
too far down his nose,
would turn the thin pages,
crackling like the Sunday chicken
in Mother's kitchen, while
his easy voice told us wonderful tales;
more wonderful than the words alone
could ever do.
Then, slowly,
his voice would linger,
shorten,
and nod off
in his own
inaudible wisdom.
My sister would sigh in disgust,
I would playfully punch his belly,
and listen for the pages,
nearly flattening against his half-shut eyes,
to rustle in awakening.
Nap time lost,
my father would read on,
while we lay, listening, smiling
on either side.

—Anne Keiter

GIRL SITTING ALONE AT PARTY

You sit with hands folded—
A madonna, a rock.

And yet when your eyes move,
As they do,

As they cannot help doing,
Your eyes are dancers.

It is for them that the rooms below
Were darkened.

And when you go,
It is there, towards music.

Your shadow, though,
Stays with me.

It sits with hands folded, stubbornly.
It will say nothing.

It is a dark rock
Against which the sea beats.

This is that other music, to which
I embrace your shadow.

—Donald Justice

&

GIRL IN FRONT OF THE BANK

The windshield wipers clear an arc
in which you stand raincoated, blonde,
reshadowed on the bank's shiny glass

as you watch me. Your eyes are blue.
It's funny that a raincoat, belted,
buttoned, promises only you beneath—

as in a shift or woolen nightgown
sexier than lace. If lampposts (green)
were trees, I'd have you in the grass

and daisies—but here is all concrete.
No absolutes. Preparing to go off
into our separate lives, we are merely

by the moment's imagination
lovers, and see (we carefully look)
each other, with a fire, and glasses,

in shadowy chambers of the perfect grace.
We ignore what we might do
—wiser than Adam and Eve in flowers—

committed elsewhere, nowhere, longing.
I don't leap out. You wait your bus.
Yet, girl, we hold love's possibility.

—Robert Wallace

&

MY SONS

I'll teach my sons
        the same as me—LOOK
at those girls on the bus to work
        intimations of real
warm bloodgiving flesh,
        comfortable, moving
beneath the cloth . . .
. . . to fill our days with beauty
from whatever faucet's available.

—Ron Loewinsohn

MARRIAGE CONTRACT

No one spells out the unwritten agreement,
the fine unphrased concessions made
between the two parties.

She, party of the first part,
protects him from seeing his own face
on mirrored walls. She covers the glass
with delicate pictures, subtle drawings
which equal his imagined self as he
lumbers through halls breaking china,
shattering delicate glass and smiling
a ludicrous grin at dreams of himself.

He, party of the second part, accepts
his role and plays the crude but sensitive man.
In the night he practices his gait,
lumbering through dreams of flowers,
breaking the stems of trees, hiding
his own soft face like mollusc flesh
within the grinning shell
he's sworn by secret law to wear.

—Vern Rutsala

&

THE PERFECT HUSBAND

He tells you when you've got on too much lipstick,
And helps you with your girdle when your hips stick.

—Ogden Nash

ELEGY

Her face like a rain-beaten stone on the day she rolled
off
With the dark hearse, and enough flowers for an
alderman,—
And so she was, in her way, Aunt Tilly.

Sighs, sighs, who says they have sequence?
Between the spirit and the flesh,—what war?
She never knew;
For she asked no quarter and gave none,
Who sat with the dead when the relatives left,
Who fed and tended the infirm, the mad, the epileptic,
And, with a harsh rasp of a laugh at herself,
Faced up to the worst.

I recall how she harried the children away
all the late summer
From the one beautiful thing in her yard, the peachtree;
How she kept the wizened, the fallen,
the misshapen for herself,
And picked and pickled the best, to be left
on rickety doorsteps.

And yet she died in agony,
Her tongue, at the last, thick, black as an ox's.

Terror of cops, bill collectors, betrayers of the poor,—
I see you in some celestial supermarket,
Moving serenely among the leeks and cabbages,
Probing the squash,
Bearing down, with two steady eyes,
On the quaking butcher.

—*Theodore Roethke*

&

ELEGY FOR A WOMAN WHO REMEMBERED EVERYTHING

She knew the grades of all her neighbors' children,
the birthdays
Of cousins once removed, the addresses of friends
who had moved
Once at least—to the coordinates of cemeteries
Where their choice views lay over their front feet.

If it had a name or a number, she missed nothing:
A mailman's neck size, the unpronounceable village
where the dentist's
Wife's half-sister ruined her kneecap, an almanac of
sutures,
The ingredients of five thousand immemorial crocks.

Her ears were as perfectly pitched as a piano-tunner's.
In the maze of total recall, she met with amazement
The data of each new day, absorbed the absorbing
facts and the absorbent
Fictions of everyone's life but her own, losing the
thread

Of that thin tracery in dialogue hauled back verbatim
Through years leaning cracked and crooked against
each other.
Death, you may dictate as rapidly or incoherently
as you wish:
She will remember everything about you.
Nothing will escape her.

—David Wagoner

GLASS

Words of a poem should be glass
But glass so simple-subtle its shape
Is nothing but the shape of what it holds.

A glass spun for itself is empty,
Brittle, at best Venetian trinket.
Embossed glass hides the poem or its absence.

Words should be looked through, should be windows.
The best word were invisible.
The poem is the thing the poet thinks.

If the impossible were not
And if the glass, only the glass,
Could be removed, the poem would remain.

—Robert Francis

&

THEORY OF POETRY

Know the word by heart
Or never know it!
Let the pedant stand apart—
Nothing he can name will show it:
Also him of intellectual art.
None know it
Till they know the world by heart.

Take heart then, poet!

—Archibald MacLeish

USES OF POETRY

Love poems they read
Were work of an aging man
Alone and celibate
Who published them in joy
Of his craftsman's skill,
How they folded into each other.

Many a lust-starched boy
Read them aloud to his girl
Till her widening eyes darkened
Till her breath trembled thin
Till the boy threw down the book
And they folded into each other.

—*Winfield Townley Scott*

FOR POETS

Stay beautiful
but dont stay down underground too
long
Dont turn into a mole
or a worm
or a root
or a stone

Come on out into the sunlight
Breathe in trees
Knock out mountains
Commune with snakes
& be the very hero of birds

Dont forget to poke your head up
& blink
think
Walk all around
Swim upstream

Dont forget to fly

—*Al Young*

Acknowledgments

Permission to reprint copyrighted poems is gratefully acknowledged to the following:

Atheneum Publishers, Inc., for "Love Letters, Unmailed" and "Reply to the Question" from *Rainbow Writing,* Copyright © 1976 by Eve Merriam. "The Windows" and "White Summer Flower" from *The Compass Flower,* Copyright © 1977 by W. S. Merwin. "Burning Love Letters" from *The Toy Fair,* Copyright © 1954 by Howard Moss, and from *Selected Poems,* Copyright © 1971 by Howard Moss; "Going to Sleep in the Country" from *Finding Them Lost,* Copyright © 1965 by Howard Moss, and from *Selected Poems,* Copyright © 1971 by Howard Moss.

Black Sparrow Press, for "Crows" from *When Things Get Tough on Easy Street,* Copyright © 1978 by Tom Clark. "The Old Men" and "On a Sunday" from *Poems 1937–1975, Volume II of the Complete Poems of Charles Reznikoff,* Copyright © 1977 by Marie Syrkin Reznikoff.

Bolt & Watson, Ltd., for "Along the River" by D. J. Enright.

George Braziller, Inc., New York, for "Accomplishments" by Cynthia MacDonald.

Henry Carlile, for "Grandmother" from *The Rough-Hewn Table,* University of Missouri Press, 1971, Copyright © Henry Carlile.

Chatto and Windus Ltd. (for Canada), for "Gnat on My Paper" and "To Evan" from *Collected Poems 1930–1976* by Richard Eberhart.

Curtis Brown, Ltd., for "The Sound of Night" from *Halfway* by Maxine Kumin, Copyright © 1961 by Maxine Kumin. "Radar" from *Something of the Sea* by Alan Ross.

Cut Bank Magazine, University of Montana, for "The Child in the Rug" by John Haines.

Andre Deutsch Ltd., (**for Canada**), for "Radar" from *Something of the Sea* by Alan Ross.

Doubleday and Company, Inc., for "On a Child Who Lived One Minute" from *Nude Descending a Staircase,* Copyright © 1958 by X. J. Kennedy (first published in *The New Yorker*). "Double Feature," Copyright 1942 by Commonweal Publishing Company, Inc.; "Elegy" from *The Collected Poems of Theodore Roethke;* "My Dim-Wit Cousin," Copyright 1941 by Theodore Roethke; "Night Crow," Copyright 1944 by The Saturday Review Association, Inc., from *The Collected Poems of Theodore Roethke.* "Gooseberries" from *Chihuahua,* Copyright © 1976 by Peter Wild (first published in *The Little Magazine,* Copyright © 1973).

Philip Dow, for "Early Morning."

E. P. Dutton & Company, Inc., for "Lines for a Friend Who Left" and "On the House of a Friend" from *The Zigzag Walk* by John Logan, Copyright © 1963, 1964, 1965, 1966, 1967, 1968, 1969 by John Logan.

The Ecco Press, for "Ode to a Dead Dodge," by David McElroy from *Making It Simple,* Copyright © 1975 by David McElroy.

George Economou, for "Poem for a Suicide," © George Economou.

Faber and Faber Limited (**for Canada**), for "Daybreak" and "To My Daughter" from *Collected Poems* by Stephen Spender.

Farrar, Straus & Giroux, Inc., for "A War" and "Moving" from *The Complete Poems* by Randall Jarrell. Copyright 1948, 1951, by Mrs. Randall Jarrell, Copyright renewed © 1976, 1979 by Mrs. Randall Jarrell.

Goldenmood Rainbow, for "Packard" by David Barker.

Harcourt Brace Jovanovich, Inc., for "The Grandmother" from *Farming: A Handbook* by Wendell Berry, Copyright © 1969 by Wendell Berry.

Holt, Rinehart and Winston, Publishers, for "For Poets" from *The Song Turning Back Into Itself* by Al Young, Copyright © 1965, 1966, 1967, 1968, 1970, 1971 by Al Young.

Houghton Mifflin Company, for "Theory of Poetry" from *New and Collected Poems 1917–1976* by Archibald MacLeish, Copyright © 1976 by Archibald MacLeish.

Indiana University Press, for "Elegy for a Woman Who Remembered Everything" and "House-Hunting" from *Collected Poems 1956–1976* by David Wagoner, Copyright © 1976 by Indiana University Press.

Anne Keiter, for "Sunday Funnies," Copyright © by Anne Keiter.

Alfred A. Knopf, Inc., for "Poem," Copyright 1932 and renewed 1960 by Langston Hughes, "Suicide's Note," Copyright 1926 by Alfred A. Knopf, Inc. and renewed 1954 by Langston Hughes, from *Selected Poems.* "Going In," "Insomnia" and "The Root Canal" from *The Twelve-Spoked Wheel* by Marge Piercy, Copyright © 1978 by Marge Piercy. "Insomnia the Gem of the Ocean," Copyright © 1972 by John Updike, "Sunday Rain," Copyright © 1971 by John Updike, from *Tossing and Turning.*

Little, Brown and Co., for "The Canary," "Old Men," "The Kitten," and "The Perfect Husband" from *Verses From 1929 On* by Ogden Nash, Copyright 1940 by The Curtis Publishing Company; Copyright 1931, 1949 by Ogden Nash. "Lament for the Non-Swimmers" and "To the Fly in My Drink" from *In Broken Country: Poems* by David Wagoner, Copyright © 1979 by David Wagoner ("To the Fly in My Drink" first published in *Carolina Quarterly;* "Lament for The Non-Swimmers" first published in *The Atlantic Monthly*).

Liveright Publishing Corporation, for "if there are any heavens" from *ViVa* by e. e. cummings, edited by George James Firmage, Copyright 1931, 1959 by E. E. Cummings, Copyright © 1973, 1979 by Nancy T. Andrews, Copyright © 1973, 1979 by George James Firmage. "Those Winter Sundays" from *Angle of Ascent, New and Selected Poems* by Robert Hayden, Copyright © 1975, 1972, 1970, 1966 by Robert Hayden.

Ron Loewinsohn, for "My Sons."

Louisiana State University Press, for "A City Graveyard," "Children Not Kept at Home," and "Insomnia" from *Angel Fire* by Joyce Carol Oates, Copyright © 1973.

Dick Lourie, for "Ann's House."

Howard Nemerov, for "Dandelions" and "Going Away" from *The Collected Poems of Howard Nemerov,* The University of Chicago Press, 1977.

New Directions Publishing Corp., for "A Day Begins" from *The Sorrow Dance* by Denise Levertov, Copyright © 1966 by Denise Levertov Goodman. "The Red-Wing Blackbird" from *Collected Later Poems of William Carlos Williams,* Copyright 1948 by William Carlos Williams.

The New Republic, Inc., for "This Is a Poem to My Son Peter" by Peter Meinke, Copyright © 1971 by The New Republic, Inc.

W. W. Norton & Company, Inc., for "Bay Bank" from *Collected Poems, 1951–1971,* by A. R. Ammons, Copyright © 1972 by A. R. Ammons. "Love Letter" and "Poet" from *The Five Stages of Grief* by Linda Pastan, Copyright © 1978 by Linda Pastan. "Moving in Winter" from *Poems, Selected and New, 1950–1974,* by Adrienne Rich, Copyright © 1975, 1973, 1971, 1969, 1966 by W. W. Norton & Company, Inc. and Copyright © 1967, 1963, 1962, 1961, 1960, 1959, 1958, 1957, 1956, 1955, 1954, 1953, 1952, 1951 by Adrienne Rich.

Oxford University Press, for "Gnat on My Paper" and "To Evan" from *Collected Poems 1930–1976* by Richard Eberhart, Copyright 1960, 1976 by Richard Eberhart. "War Story" from *The Apple Barrel* by John Stallworthy, Copyright © 1963 Oxford University Press.

Ploughshares, Inc., for "Wind Flowers" by Margo Lockwood, "Portrait of My Mother on Her Wedding Day" by Celia Gilbert, and "Anthony" by Jane Shore, Copyright © 1980, Ploughshares, Inc.

Poetry, for "The Poet's Farewell to His Teeth" from *The Rainbow*

Grocery by William Dickey, also by permission of the author (originally printed in *Poetry,* July 1972, Copyright © 1972 by The Modern Poetry Association).

Ralph Pomeroy, for "Gone," "To My Father" and "Near Drowning" from *In the Financial District,* Macmillan Publishing Company, Inc.

Random House, Inc., for "The Poet" from *An Ordinary Woman* by Lucille Clifton, Copyright © 1974 by Lucille Clifton. "Buick," Copyright 1942 and renewed 1970 by Karl Jay Shapiro; "The Glutton," Copyright 1942 by Karl Jay Shapiro; "Interlude," Copyright 1944 and renewed 1972 by Karl Jay Shapiro; "The Leg," Copyright 1944 by Karl Jay Shapiro, from *Collected Poems, 1940–1978* by Karl Shapiro. "Daybreak," Copyright 1942 and renewed 1970 by Stephen Spender; "To My Daughter," Copyright © 1955 by Stephen Spender, from *Collected Poems, 1928–1953* by Stephen Spender. "Boy Wandering in Simms' Valley" Copyright © 1978 by Robert Penn Warren.

Dan Saxon, for "Walking in the Rain."

Lindsay B. Scott, for "To L.B.S." by Winfield Townley Scott.

Estate of W. T. Scott, for "Uses of Poetry" by Winfield Townley Scott.

Charles Scribner's Sons, for "After the Dentist" and "The Secret in the Cat" from *The Guess and Spell Coloring Book,* Copyright © 1976 by May Swenson.

Susan Sherman, for "Three Moments," Copyright © 1968 by Susan Sherman.

Solo Press, Atascadero, California, for "Abandoned Farmhouse" and "In a Country Cemetery in Iowa" by Ted Kooser.

Southern Poetry Review, for "I Show the Daffodils to the Retarded Kids" by Constance Sharp.

Stephenson Harwood (for Canada), for "A Post-Mortem" by Siegfried Sassoon.

The University of Chicago Press, for "Nightfall" from *Olson's Penny Arcade,* Copyright 1963, 1975 by Elder Olson.

The University of Massachusetts Press, for "Bouquets," "Boy at a Certain Age," "Cats" and "The House Remembers" from *Robert Francis: Collected Poems, 1936–1976,* Copyright © 1970, 1974 by Robert Francis.

The University of Missouri Press, for "My Teeth" and "The Gift" from *Dancing on the Edges of Knives* by Ed Ochester, also by permission of the author, Copyright 1973 by Ed Ochester.

The University of Nebraska, for "Disintegration" and "Wonders of the World" by Richard Shelton, reprinted from *Pebble #12.*

The University of Pittsburgh Press, for "Letter to a Dead Father" and "Youth" from *You Can't Have Everything* by Richard Shelton, Copyright © 1975 by Richard Shelton.

Vanderbilt University Press, for "The Amputation" from *Seeds As They Fall* by Helen Sorrells, 1971.

Viking Penguin, Inc., for "Crows" from *Margins* by Philip Booth, Copyright © 1969 by Philip Booth. "A Post-Mortem" from *Sequences* by Siefried Sassoon, Published by Viking Press, Inc., 1957.

Mark Vinz, for "The Children" from *Winter Promises,* Bk Mk Press, Copyright © 1975 by Mark Vinz.

Robert Wallace, for "Girl in Front of the Bank" and "The Two Old Gentlemen," Copyright © 1965 by Robert Wallace.

Wallace & Sheil Agency, Inc., for "Barbie Doll" from *To Be of Use,* Doubleday, 1973, Copyright © 1973 by Marge Piercy.

Wesleyan University Press, for "Swimmer," Copyright © 1953, and "Glass," Copyright © 1949 by Robert Francis, from *The Orb Weaver* by Robert Francis. "My Grandmother Had Bones," Copyright © 1972, and "Strawberries," Copyright © 1973 by Judith Hemschemeyer, from

I Remember the Room Was Filled with Light by Judith Hemschemeyer Rosenfeld. "Cardinal" from *The Blue Garden,* © by Barbara Howes; "Cat on Couch" from *Light and Dark,* © 1955 by Barbara Howes; "The Dressmaker's Dummy as Scarecrow" from *A Private Scandal,* © by Barbara Howes; "Portrait of the Boy as Artist" from *Light and Dark,* © 1956 by Barbara Howes. "Song," © 1953 by Donald Justice, and "Sonnet to My Father," © 1959 by Donald Justice, from *The Summer Anniversaries;* "Girl Sitting Alone at Party," and "Ode to a Dressmaker's Dummy," from *Night Light,* © 1967 by Donald Justice. "Bijou," Copyright © 1960, "Marriage Contract," Copyright © 1959, "Sunday," Copyright © 1964 and "The Fat Man," Copyright © 1963 by Vern Rutsala, from *The Window* by Vern Rutsala.

Keith Wilson, for "The Arrival of My Mother" from *While Dancing Feet Shatter the Earth,* Utah State University Press, Copyright © 1978 by Keith Wilson.

P. Wolny, for "From a Birch" and "Separation."

Celeste Turner Wright, for "Yugoslav Cemetery" from *Seasoned Timber* by Celeste Turner Wright, Golden Quill Press, 1977, Copyrighted.

Index of Poets

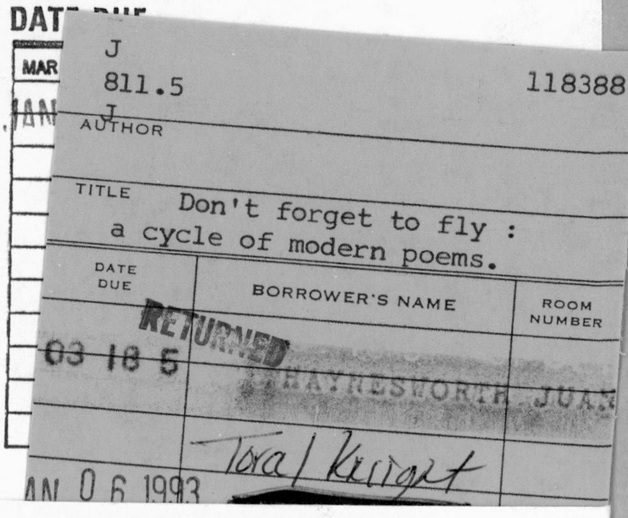